Let's Look at Apple Trees

Katie Peters

GRL Consultants,
Diane Craig and Monica Marx,
Certified Literacy Specialists

Pull Ahead READERS

Lerner Publications ◆ Minneapolis

Note from a GRL Consultant
This Pull Ahead leveled book has been carefully designed for beginning readers. A team of guided reading literacy experts has reviewed and leveled the book to ensure readers pull ahead and experience success.

Lerner Publications Company
An imprint of Lerner Publishing Group, Inc.
241 First Avenue North
Minneapolis, MN 55401 USA

For reading levels and more information, look up this title at www.lernerbooks.com.

Main body text set in Memphis Pro 24/39
Typeface provided by Linotype.

Photo Acknowledgments
The images in this book are used with the permission of: © Boonchuay1970/iStockphoto, pp. 4 (seeds), 5 (seeds), 16 (seeds); © Carmen Hauser/iStockphoto, pp. 8, 9; © Chet_W/iStockphoto, pp. 4 (soil background), 5 (soil background), 16 (soil background); © Cimmerian/iStockphoto, pp. 12, 13, 16 (blossom); © ligora/iStockphoto, pp. 10, 11, 16 (bud); © redstallion/iStockphoto, pp. 14, 15; © Sergey_Sizov/iStockphoto, pp. 6, 7, 16 (sprout); © Sieboldianus/iStockphoto, p. 3.

Front cover: © S847/iStockphoto

Library of Congress Cataloging-in-Publication Data

Names: Peters, Katie, author.
Title: Let's look at apple trees / Katie Peters.
Description: Minneapolis : Lerner Publications, [2021] | Series: Plant life cycles (pull ahead readers - nonfiction) | Audience: Ages 4–7 | Audience: Grades K–1 | Summary: "Have you ever seen an apple blossom? Carefully leveled text and engaging photos show emergent readers what apples look like while they are growing in an orchard. Pairs with the fiction title Baking Apples."— Provided by publisher.
Identifiers: LCCN 2019046321 (print) | LCCN 2019046322 (ebook) | ISBN 9781541590205 (library binding) | ISBN 9781728403113 (paperback) | ISBN 9781728400730 (ebook)
Subjects: LCSH: Apples—Life cycles—Juvenile literature.
Classification: LCC SB363 .P388 2021 (print) | LCC SB363 (ebook) | DDC 634/.11—dc23

LC record available at https://lccn.loc.gov/2019046321
LC ebook record available at https://lccn.loc.gov/2019046322

Manufactured in the United States of America
4-1011364-48074-5/31/2024

Contents

Let's Look at Apple Trees

Look at the apple seeds.

Look at the apple sprout.

Look at the apple tree.

Look at the apple buds.

Look at the apple flowers.

Look at the apples.

Did You See It?

apple buds

apple flowers

apple seeds

apple sprout

Index